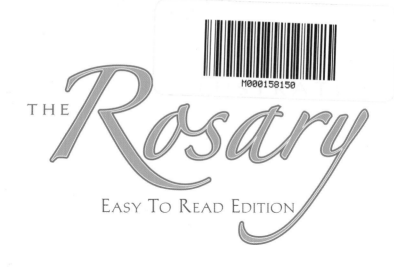

THE Rosary

EASY TO READ EDITION

Catholic™
CLASSICS

Edited by

Victor Hoagland, C.P.

Regina
Press

Nihil Obstat: Reverend Robert O. Morrisey, J.C.D.
Censor librorum
January 13th, 2003

Imprimatur: Most Reverend William Murphy
Bishop of Rockville Centre
January 15th, 2003

THE REGINA PRESS
10 Hub Drive
Melville, New York 11747

ISBN# 0-88271-684-0

Printed in Belgium.

The Rosary of the Blessed Virgin Mary

"To recite the rosary is nothing other than to contemplate the face of Christ with Mary."

Pope John Paul II

In his letter "Rosarium Virginis Mariae" October 16, 2002, Pope John Paul II expressed his esteem for a method of praying that has nourished the faith of generations of Christians. The pope called on Catholics – and other Christians as well – to pray the rosary and enter "the school of Mary," who knew Jesus Christ so well as his mother and who was his closest disciple.

Though it is not mandatory, the pope also suggested that five mysteries be added to the traditional fifteen. He called them "Luminous Mysteries," or the Mysteries of Light, which include the mysteries of Christ's public ministry between his Baptism and his Passion. While leaving the use of these mysteries "to the freedom of individuals and communities," Pope John Paul suggested that they could help make the prayer more deeply centered in the life of Christ.

This book includes the Luminous Mysteries, taken from a period of Jesus' life when he revealed himself as "the light of the world," and incorporates them into the fifteen traditional mysteries.

The Rosary and the Scriptures

Pope John Paul II also recommended the use of scriptural verses to accompany each mystery of the rosary in order to deepen the scriptural dimension of this prayer. This book offers short scriptural verses as well as meditations to highlight each mystery.

The Rosary:
Where Did It Come From?

Praying the rosary well is more important than knowing its history, yet knowing the origins of the prayer can teach us much about it.

The beginnings of the rosary are found in the early Christian practice of reciting the 150 psalms from the bible, either daily or weekly, as a way of prayer. Those unable to recite the psalms began to recite 150 payers, mainly the

Our Father, 150 times, often using beads to count the prayers. By medieval times the custom of saying "Paternoster" beads (the Latin for Our Father) was common in many countries of Europe. While saying the prayers it was customary to meditate on the mysteries of the life of Jesus, from his birth to his resurrection.

The rosary in its present form arose in late medieval Christianity when Mary, the Mother of Jesus, was seen as a guide to the mysteries of her Son. A decade of prayers called the Hail Mary was preceded by the Our Father. Meditation on the mysteries of Christ remained at the heart of the prayer.

Through the centuries, saints like St. Dominic, many of the popes, as well as countless ordinary Christians have found the rosary to be a school of prayer and a source of spiritual blessing. It is both simple and profound. Not beyond anyone's reach, its repeated words bring peace to the soul. And the mysteries of Jesus that it recalls are also meant to be repeated on our own. We ask to "imitate what they contain and obtain what they promise, through Christ our Lord."

The Hail Mary

The Hail Mary evolved as a prayer from the devotion of medieval men and women who saw Mary, the mother to Jesus, as the great witness to His life, death and resurrection. Its earliest form was the greeting made to Mary by the Angel Gabriel:

Hail Mary, full of grace, the Lord is with you
Luke 1:28

Over time the greeting given to Mary by her cousin Elizabeth was added:

Blessed are you among women
and blessed is the fruit of your womb.
Luke 1:42

Finally by the 15th century, the remainder of the prayer appeared:

Holy Mary, mother of God, pray for us sinners now and at the hour of our death.

The prayer calls upon Mary, full of grace and close to her Son, to intercede for us sinners now and at the time our death. We share her as a mother with St. John to whom Jesus entrusted her, when on Calvary He said, "Behold your mother." She will always bring Christ into our life. We trust her to care for us as she cared for the newly married couple at Cana in Galilee. We can go to her in our need.

By the end of the 16th century the practice of saying 150 Hail Marys in series or decades of 10 was popular among many ordinary Christian people. The mysteries of the life, death and resurrection of Jesus, contained in the Joyful, Sorrowful and Glorious Mysteries, were remembered during these prayers.

Why We Pray the Rosary

The rosary is a special way of praying. As we recite the prayers of the rosary, we think about certain stories in the lives of Jesus and Mary. These stories are called "mysteries". We use rosary beads to help us keep count of the prayers and the mysteries.

How to Pray the Rosary

The complete rosary consists of twenty decades, but it is further divided into four distinct parts, the Joyful, the Luminous, the Sorrowful, and the Glorious Mysteries, each containing five decades.

To say the rosary, begin by making the sign of the cross and saying the Apostles' Creed on the crucifix, one Our Father on the first bead, three Hail Marys on the next three beads, and then a Glory Be to the Father. When this is finished, meditate upon the first mystery, say an Our Father, ten Hail Marys, and one Glory Be to the Father. The first decade is now completed, and to finish the rosary proceed in the same manner until all five decades have been said. When this is done, say one Hail Holy Queen.

As a prayer of faith, the rosary usually begins with two basic summaries of faith: the Sign of the Cross and the Creed. These prayers invite us to believe in God, the Father, the Son, and Holy Spirit, and to remember God's plan of salvation proclaimed in the scriptures.

The rosary is made up of decades of prayers. A decade of the rosary consists of an Our Father prayed before ten Hail Marys. At the end of a decade the prayer "Glory be to the Father, and to the Son, and to the Holy Spirit" is said. Most rosaries have five decades of beads.

6.
Meditate on 3rd Mystery, saying the "Our Father," ten "Hail Marys" and the "Glory Be."

7.
Meditate on 4th Mystery, saying the "Our Father," ten "Hail Marys" and the "Glory Be."

5.
Meditate on 2nd Mystery, saying the "Our Father," ten "Hail Marys" and the "Glory Be."

8.
Meditate on 5th Mystery, saying the "Our Father," ten "Hail Marys" and the "Glory Be.""

4.
Meditate on 1st Mystery, saying the "Our Father," ten "Hail Marys" and the "Glory Be."

9.
Concluding prayer, "Hail Holy Queen"

3.
Say three "Hail Marys" and the "Glory Be."

2.
Say the "Our Father".

1.
Make the Sign of the Cross, say the Apostles' Creed.

Prayers of the Rosary

The Sign of the Cross

In the name of the Father, † and of the Son, and of the Holy Spirit. Amen.

The Apostles' Creed

I believe in God, the Father Almighty, Creator of heaven and earth; and in Jesus Christ, His only Son, our Lord, who was conceived by the Holy Spirit; born of the Virgin Mary, suffered under Pontius Pilate, was crucified, died and was buried. He descended into hell; the third day He rose again from the dead; He ascended into heaven, sitteth at the right hand God the Father Almighty; from thence He shall come to judge the living and the dead. I believe in the Holy Spirit, the Holy Catholic Church, the communion of Saints, the forgiveness of sins, the resurrection of the body, and life everlasting. Amen.

The Our Father

Our Father who art in heaven, hallowed be Thy name; Thy kingdom come; Thy will be done on earth as it is in heaven. Give us this day our daily bread; and forgive us our trespasses as we forgive those who trespass against us. And lead us not into temptation; but deliver us from evil. Amen.

The Hail Mary

Hail Mary, full of grace, the Lord is with you; Blessed are you among women, and blessed is the fruit of your womb, Jesus. Holy Mary, Mother of God, pray for us sinners, now and at the hour our death. Amen.

Glory Be to the Father

Glory be to the Father, and to the Son, and to the Holy Spirit; as it was in the beginning, is now, and ever shall be, world without end. Amen.

The Hail, Holy Queen

Hail, holy Queen, Mother of Mercy! Our life, our sweetness, and our hope! To thee do we cry, poor banished children of Eve; to thee do we send up our sighs, mourning and weeping in this valley of tears. Turn, then, most gracious advocate, thine eyes of mercy toward us; and after this our exile show unto us the blessed fruit of thy womb Jesus; O clement, O loving, O sweet Virgin Mary.

V. Pray for us, O holy Mother of God.

R. That we may be made worthy of the promises of Christ.

The Five Joyful Mysteries

Mondays and Saturdays

FIRST JOYFUL MYSTERY
The Annunciation
The Angel Gabriel tells Mary that she is to be the Mother of God.

SECOND JOYFUL MYSTERY
The Visitation
The Blessed Virgin pays a visit to her cousin Elizabeth.

THIRD JOYFUL MYSTERY
The Birth of Jesus
The Infant Jesus is born in a stable at Bethlehem.

FOURTH JOYFUL MYSTERY
Presentation of Jesus in the Temple
The Blessed Virgin presents the Child Jesus to Simeon in the Temple.

FIFTH JOYFUL MYSTERY
Finding the Child Jesus in the Temple
Jesus is lost for three days, and the Blessed Mother finds Him in the Temple.

1st Joyful Mystery
The Annunciation

The Angel Gabriel
appears to Mary,
announcing she is to
be the Mother of God.

5th Joyful Mystery
*The Finding in
the Temple*

The Blessed
Mother finds
Jesus in the
Temple.

2nd Joyful Mystery
The Visitation

Elizabeth greets Mary:
"Blessed art Thou
among women and
blessed is the fruit of
Thy womb!"

4th Joyful Mystery
The Presentation

3rd Joyful Mystery
The Nativity

The Blessed
Mother presents
the Child Jesus in
the Temple.

The Virgin
Mary gives birth
to the Redeemer
of the World.

Bartolome Esteban Murillo. *The Annunciation*,
Prado, Madrid, Spain

FIRST JOYFUL MYSTERY

The Annunciation

Then the angel said to her, "Do not be afraid, Mary, for you have found favor with God. Behold, you will conceive in your womb and bear a son, and you shall name him Jesus."

Luke 1, 30-31

Meditation

Nor was Mary afraid to do God's will. The angel left her, but she was not afraid, even as she faced Joseph's initial doubt, even though she did not fully understand it all. She trusted even through the birth in a poor stable, through the silent years at Nazareth, the mysterious years of Jesus' ministry and the darkest hours of His passion and death.

Mary believed God's purpose for her, even though she did not always understand.

One Our Father, ten Hail Marys and one Glory Be to the Father.

Raphael (Raffaello Sanzio of Urbino). *The Visitation*,
Prado, Madrid, Spain

SECOND JOYFUL MYSTERY
The Visitation

When Elizabeth heard Mary's greeting, the infant leaped in her womb, and Elizabeth, filled with the holy Spirit, cried out in a loud voice and said, "Most blessed are you among women, and blessed is the fruit of your womb."

Luke 1, 41-42

Meditation

Such a simple thing: two cousins visit! One blesses the other. Mary, with the mighty Child within her, makes Elizabeth's unborn infant leap for joy. And the elder Elizabeth speaks words of praise to the younger Mary. "Blessed are you..."

A simple visit between two people, yet blessings are exchanged and the two strengthened by God's grace.

One Our Father, ten Hail Marys and one Glory Be to the Father.

Philippe de Champaigne. *The Adoration of the Shepherds,*
Wallace Collection, London, UK

THIRD JOYFUL MYSTERY

The Birth of Jesus

"And she gave birth to her first-born son. She wrapped him in swaddling clothes and laid him in a manger, because there was no room for them in the inn."

Luke 2, 7

Meditation

A Child is born for us! In the poorest of places, a stable. With nothing of his own, Jesus Christ was born. He would always be poor, as one of us, and the poor always found a welcome near Him. The shepherds came at the angel's call, leading their sheep. And they returned singing for joy. Later, the blind, the lame and the deaf came. Jesus welcomed them, too. Those possessed by demons, those haunted by fears came; their spirits were lifted and they felt their hearts soar.

One Our Father, ten Hail Marys and one Glory Be to the Father.

Rembrandt Harmensz. *Simeon and Hannah in the Temple*, Hamburg Kunsthalle, Hamburg, Germany

FOURTH JOYFUL MYSTERY

Presentation of Jesus in the Temple

When the days were completed for their purification according to the law of Moses, they took him up to Jerusalem to present him to the Lord.

Luke 2, 22

Meditation

For Mary and Joseph the time came, shortly after Jesus' birth, to present Him in the temple to God. The time came too for the old man Simeon and the old woman Anna, waiting and praying so long. Waiting in the temple many years, they were hoping God's promises to their people would be fulfilled. The day the tiny Child came, their waiting was rewarded.

"Now dismiss your servant in peace, O Lord, because my eyes have seen your salvation," Simeon said as he took the child in his arms.

One Our Father, ten Hail Marys and one Glory Be to the Father.

Rembrandt Harmensz. *The Twelve Year Old Jesus in front of the Scribes,*
Hamburg Kunsthalle, Hamburg, Germany

FIFTH JOYFUL MYSTERY
Finding the Child Jesus in the Temple

"After three days they found him in the temple, sitting in the midst of the teachers, listening to them and asking them questions."

Luke 3, 46

Meditation

A special joy comes from finding what we thought lost or seeing what we were anxious about turn out for the best. The Joyful Mysteries of the Rosary are about such joys: The joys that follow fear, sorrow, struggle and uncertainty.

Look at Mary and Joseph searching for their lost son for three days. Finding Him, their sorrow turns to joy. The lesson is simple: God makes our hearts for joy and will not let us lose treasures that truly matter. Our joy comes from seeking Him.

One Our Father, ten Hail Marys, one Glory Be to the Father and one Hail Holy Queen.

The Five Luminous Mysteries

Thursdays

FIRST LUMINOUS MYSTERY
The Baptism of Christ
Jesus is baptized in the Jordan River by
John the Baptist.

SECOND LUMINOUS MYSTERY
The Wedding at Cana
Jesus attends a wedding at Cana in
Galilee, where he turns water into wine.

THIRD LUMINOUS MYSTERY
The Proclamation of the Kingdom of God
Jesus goes through the towns and cities
of his own country proclaiming God's
Kingdom and helping the poor.

FOURTH LUMINOUS MYSTERY
The Transfiguration
Jesus leads his friends up a high mountain,
where they see him shining in glorious light.

FIFTH LUMINOUS MYSTERY
The Institution of the Holy Eucharist
At supper with his friends before he dies,
Jesus gives himself to them in bread
and wine.

1st Luminous Mystery
Baptism of Christ

Jesus is baptized in the River Jordan by John the Baptist.

5th Luminous Mystery
Institution of Holy Eucharist

At supper with his friends before he dies, Jesus gives himself to them in bread and wine.

2nd Luminous Mystery
Wedding at Cana

Jesus attends a wedding at Cana in Galilee, where he turns water into wine.

4th Luminous Mystery
Transfiguration

Jesus leads friends up a high mountain, where they see him shining in glorious light.

3rd Luminous Mystery
Proclamation of Kingdom of God

Jesus goes through the towns and cities of his own country proclaiming God's Kingdom and helping the poor.

Alessandro Allori. *The Baptism of Christ,*
Galleria dell' Accademia, Florence, Italy

FIRST LUMINOUS MYSTERY

The Baptism of Jesus

It happened in those days that Jesus came from Nazareth of Galilee and was baptized in the Jordan by John.

Mark 1, 9

Meditation

Usually the story of Jesus begins with his birth in Bethlehem, but New Testament sources such as the Gospel of Mark begin his story with his Baptism. After that, Jesus "went about doing good works and healing all who were in the grip of the devil, and God was with him." (Acts 10,38)

From the heavens, God says, "You are my beloved Son; in you I am well pleased. (Mark 1,11) Jesus is God's only Son. But in Baptism his followers become children of God too. With no claim of our own, we are invited by him into God's family and we go in his name to bring goodness and healing to the world in which we live.

One Our Father, ten Hail Marys and one Glory Be to the Father.

Bartolome Esteban Murillo. *The Marriage Feast at Cana,*
The Barber Institute of Fine Arts, University of Birmingham

SECOND LUMINOUS MYSTERY
The Wedding at Cana

On the third day there was a wedding in Cana in Galilee, and the mother of Jesus was there.

John 2,1

Meditation

John's Gospel states that Jesus' public ministry began at a wedding feast that was heading for failure. The wine was running out, which meant the joy of the celebration would be dampened and the couple and their families would be embarrassed.

By changing water into wine, Jesus saved the day. His first miracle brought joy to a group of men and women. In fact, this is why he came: to bring "great joy to all people."

One Our Father, ten Hail Marys and one Glory Be to the Father.

Bartolome Esteban Murillo. *Christ at the Pool of Bethesda,*
National Gallery, London, UK

THIRD LUMINOUS MYSTERY

The Proclamation of the Kingdom of God

He went around all of Galilee, teaching in their synagogues, proclaiming the gospel of the kingdom, and curing every disease and illness among the people.

Matthew 4, 23

Meditation

After his Baptism in the Jordan, Jesus left the quiet safety of Nazareth to preach the Good News about the Kingdom. Crowds surrounded him as he went through Galilee, and he lifted their hearts with his words.

"I am the light of the world," he said, and he told them to let their light shine before all. "I am the resurrection and the life," he said, and he promised that those who believe in him would live, even though they die. "I am among you as one who serves, " he said, and he healed the sick and the troubled. "I am the good shepherd," he said, "and I am willing to die for the sheep." John 10, 11

One Our Father, ten Hail Marys and one Glory Be to the Father.

Guiseppe Cesari. *The Transfiguration*,
Ferens Art Gallery, Hull City Museums and Art Galleries, UK

FOURTH LUMINOUS MYSTERY
The Transfiguration

"About eight days after he said this, he took Peter, John, and James and went up the mountain to pray. While he was praying his face changed in appearance and his clothing became dazzling white."

Luke 9, 28-29

Meditation

On the way to Jerusalem where he would be crucified, Jesus told his disciples of his coming sufferings and death. They were deeply saddened. To raise their spirits, Jesus took them up a mountain and he was transfigured before them to show that God's glory endures, even in life's saddest moments.

Even now, God's glory shines in the darkest places of our lives, if we hold them up to the light of faith. Even now, we are given intimations, brief encounters, transfigurations of a lesser kind, as we confront the mystery of suffering.

One Our Father, ten Hail Marys and one Glory Be to the Father.

Gaudenzio Ferrari. *The Last Supper, detail of Christ,*
Santa Maria della Passione, Milan, Italy

FIFTH LUMINOUS MYSTERY
The Institution of the Holy Eucharist

Jesus said to them, "I am the bread of life; whoever comes to me will never hunger, and whoever believes in me will never thirst."

John 6, 35

Meditation

On the night before he died, Jesus gave his friends a lasting sign of his love for them. He gave them his body and his blood. For all the ages, he would be their bread of life. Through bread and wine, he gave them his body and blood.

One Our Father, ten Hail Marys, one Glory Be to the Father and one Hail Holy Queen.

The Five Sorrowful Mysteries
Tuesdays and Fridays

FIRST SORROWFUL MYSTERY
The Agony in the Garden
Jesus prays in the Garden of Olives and drops of blood break through His skin.

SECOND SORROWFUL MYSTERY
The Scourging of Jesus at the Pillar
Jesus is tied to a pillar and cruelly beaten with whips.

THIRD SORROWFUL MYSTERY
Jesus Is Crowned with Thorns
A crown of thorns is placed upon Jesus' head.

FOURTH SORROWFUL MYSTERY
Jesus Carries His Cross
Jesus is made to carry His cross to Calvary.

FIFTH SORROWFUL MYSTERY
The Crucifixion
Jesus is nailed to the cross, and dies for our sins.

1st Sorrowful Mystery
Agony in the Garden

At Gethsemane
Jesus prays as
He contemplates
the sins of the
World.

5th Sorrowful Mystery
The Crucifixion

Jesus is nailed to
the cross and
dies after three
hours of Agony.

2nd Sorrowful Mystery
The Scourging

Jesus is cruelly
scourged until His
mortified body could
bear no more.

4th Sorrowful Mystery
*Carrying
of the Cross*

3rd Sorrowful Mystery
*Crowning
with Thorns*

Jesus carries the
heavy cross upon
His shoulders to
Calvary.

A crown of
thorns is placed
on the head of
Jesus.

Luca Giordano. *The Prayer in the Garden*,
Hospital Tavera, Toledo, Spain

FIRST SORROWFUL MYSTERY

The Agony in the Garden

Then they came to a place named Gethsemane, and he said to his disciples, "Sit here while I pray."
Mark 14, 32

Meditation

Alone on that dark night, among the olive trees in a garden called Gethsemane, Jesus became fearful and disturbed. He could have fled, as His disciples would soon flee. But He stayed, kneeling on the ground, praying to His Father that the cup of suffering pass Him by, yet trusting He could drink it if it be God's will.

As He prayed His spirit grew stronger, and He rose to face what would come.

One Our Father, ten Hail Marys and one Glory Be to the Father.

Michelangelo Merisi da Caravaggio. *Flagellation*,
Museo e Gallerie Nazionali di Capodimonte, Naples, Italy

SECOND SORROWFUL MYSTERY

The Scourging of Jesus at the Pillar

So Pilate, wishing to satisfy the crowd, released Barabbas to them and, after he had Jesus scourged, handed him over to be crucified.

Mark 15, 15

Meditation

Seized in the garden, questioned and falsely accused, Jesus was condemned by Pilate, the Roman governor, to be crucified. He was judged a revolutionary, a danger to the people. And the first step for quick Roman justice was scourging: Jesus was lashed with a punishing whip, His body tracked by painful strokes of blood.

"By His stripes we were healed," the Prophet Isaiah said of You, O Lord.

One Our Father, ten Hail Marys and one Glory Be to the Father.

Sir Anthony van Dyck. *The Crowning with Thorns,*
Prado, Madrid, Spain

THIRD SORROWFUL MYSTERY

Jesus Is Crowned with Thorns

"They clothed him in purple and, weaving a crown of thorns, placed it on him."

Mark 15, 17

Meditation

The Roman soldiers who were to crucify Jesus called their companions to join them in a cruel act of mockery before they led Him to the place of execution. Jesus had claimed to be king; He spoke of a kingdom. Taking His own clothes from Him, the soldiers draped Him in a ragged purple cloak, the color of royalty, and put on His head a crown of sharp thorns. Then they knelt before Him, struck Him, and spat upon Him, saying, "Hail, King of the Jews!"

One Our Father, ten Hail Marys and one Glory Be to the Father.

Spanish School. *Christ Carrying the Cross*,
Louvre, Paris, France

FOURTH SORROWFUL MYSTERY

Jesus Carries His Cross

"So they took Jesus, and carrying the cross himself he went out to what is called the Place of the Skull, in Hebrew, Golgatha."

John 19, 17

Meditation

From the place of judgment, where He was scourged and mocked, Jesus was led, carrying His cross, outside Jerusalem's walls to Golgotha. Hardly able to walk, He stumbled along the narrow city streets, hurried by the soldiers who wanted a quick execution. Many along the way taunted Him. Most of His friends had deserted Him. Only a few stayed close by His side. Yet, though He seemed at the end of His strength, Jesus kept on.

One Our Father, ten Hail Marys and one Glory Be to the Father.

Diego Rodriguez de Silva y Velasquez. *Christ on the Cross*,
Prado, Madrid, Spain

FIFTH SORROWFUL MYSTERY
The Crucifixion

"Then they crucified him and divided his garments by casting lots for them to see what each should take."

Mark 15, 24

Meditation

With dreadful skill, the soldiers nailed Jesus to the cross and set it up against the dark sky. "Father, forgive them for they do not know what they are doing," He prayed. He also promised forgiveness to the thief at his side. And seeing His mother, He said to His disciple with her, "Behold, your mother." Though they might kill Him, the love that filled His life would not die. Even the hardened soldiers recognized greatness in this pitiable man. "Truly, He was God's Son!" the centurion exclaimed.

One Our Father, ten Hail Marys, one Glory Be to the Father and one Hail Holy Queen.

The Five Glorious Mysteries
Wednesdays and Sundays

FIRST GLORIOUS MYSTERY
The Resurrection of Jesus
Jesus rises from the dead, three days
after His death.

SECOND GLORIOUS MYSTERY
The Ascension of Jesus
Forty days after His death, Jesus
ascends into heaven.

THIRD GLORIOUS MYSTERY
The Descent of the Holy Spirit
Ten days after the Ascension, the Holy
Spirit comes to the apostles and the
Blessed Mother in the form of fiery tongues.

FOURTH GLORIOUS MYSTERY
The Assumption of Mary in Heaven
The Blessed Virgin dies and is
assumed into heaven.

FIFTH GLORIOUS MYSTERY
The Crowning of Mary
The Blessed Virgin is crowned Queen
of Heaven and Earth by Jesus, her Son.

1st Glorious Mystery
The Resurrection

Jesus rises
glorious
and immortal,
three days after
His death.

5th Glorious Mystery
The Coronation

Mary is gloriously
crowned Queen of
Heaven and Earth.

2nd Glorious Mystery
The Ascension

Jesus ascends into
Heaven forty days
after His
Resurrection.

4th Glorious Mystery
The Assumption

3rd Glorious Mystery
Descent of the Holy Spirit

The Blessed
Mother is united
with her Divine
Son in heaven.

The Holy
Spirit descends
upon Mary and
the Apostles.

Noel Coypel. *The Resurrection of Christ, 1700,*
Musee des Beaux-Arts, Rennes, France

FIRST GLORIOUS MYSTERY
The Resurrection of Jesus

Then the angel said to the women in reply, "Do not be afraid! I know that you are seeking Jesus the crucified. He is not here, for he has been raised just as he said. Come and see the place where he lay."

Matthew 28, 5-6

Meditation

*O*n Easter Sunday, the women coming to anoint the body of Jesus were sent away from the tomb, the place of death. "He is not here," the angel said, "He is risen."

Then Jesus appeared to His disciples, sometimes to one and other times to many. Soon even the most doubtful, like Thomas, were convinced. No, it was not a ghost or their imagination. They could touch His wounds with their hands. Jesus was risen from the dead.

One Our Father, ten Hail Marys and one Glory Be to the Father.

Jean Francois de Troy. *The Ascension*, 1721,
Musee des Beaux-Arts, Rouen, France

SECOND GLORIOUS MYSTERY
The Ascension of Jesus

"When he had said this, as they were looking on, he was lifted up, and a cloud took him from their sight."

Acts 1, 9

Meditation

After appearing to His disciples for over forty days, Jesus disappeared from their sight. The gospels see the risen Jesus having a further mission than just returning to life. He has a mission to begin a new creation.

"I go to prepare a place for you," Jesus promises His disciples at the Last Supper. Ascending into heaven, that is what He does: He prepares a place for us, new heavens and a new earth. A home that is ours because of His love for us. It is not only the world of here and now we hope for; we have a home above.

One Our Father, ten Hail Marys and one Glory Be to the Father.

Louis Galloche. *The Pentecost*,
Musee des Beaux-Arts, Nantes, France

THIRD GLORIOUS MYSTERY
The Descent of the Holy Spirit

"And they were all filled with the holy Spirit and began to speak in different tongues, as the Spirit enabled them to proclaim."

Acts 2, 4

Meditation

"*I* will not leave you orphans," Jesus told His disciples. They were to wait for the promised gift of the Father–the gift of the Holy Spirit.

So they waited in Jerusalem until the Jewish feast of Pentecost, fifty days after Easter. Then, as they were all together in one place, a strong wind and sound filled the house, and flames like tongues of fire came to rest on them. They were filled with the Holy Spirit.

The Holy Spirit is Jesus' "first gift to those who believe, to complete His work on earth and bring us the fullness of grace."

One Our Father, ten Hail Marys and one Glory Be to the Father.

Bartolome Esteban Murillo. *The Assumption of the Virgin*, 1670, Hermitage, St. Petersburg, Russia

FOURTH GLORIOUS MYSTERY

The Assumption of Mary in Heaven

"For if we believe that Jesus died and rose, so too will God, through Jesus, bring with him those who have fallen asleep."

1 Thessalonians 4, 14

Meditation

A long tradition supports our belief that Mary, the mother of Jesus, was assumed body and soul into heaven. God rewarded her for faithfully fulfilling her role as the Mother of Jesus. And so, she was brought to life after falling asleep in death. She was taken up into heaven.

We see her as a sign of what our future holds. In the words of the church's liturgy, she brings "hope and comfort for your people on their pilgrim way."

One Our Father, ten Hail Marys and one Glory Be to the Father.

Diego Rodriguez de Silva y Velasquez. *Coronation of the Virgin,*
Prado, Madrid, Spain

FIFTH GLORIOUS MYSTERY
The Crowning of Mary

"A great sign appeared in the sky, a woman clothed with the sun, with the moon under her feet, and on her head a crown of twelve stars."

Revelation 12, 1

Meditation

The mysteries of the rosary begin with a sign the Prophet Isaiah gave: "This is a sign to you: a virgin shall conceive and bear a son, and you will call His name Emmanuel, 'God with us.' " They end urging us to look heavenward, to the sign of a woman clothed in the glories of God's kingdom. Mary, because she stood loyally beside her Son, has become a powerful intercessor at the side of Christ, our heavenly king. She will be a mother to us.

One Our Father, ten Hail Marys, one Glory Be to the Father and one Hail Holy Queen.

Litany of the Blessed Virgin Mary

Lord, have mercy,
Christ, have mercy,
Lord, have mercy.
Christ, hear us.
Christ, graciously hear us.
God, the Father of heaven,
    have mercy on us.
God, the Son, Redeemer of the world,
    have mercy on us.
God, the Holy Spirit, have mercy on us.
Holy Trinity, one God,
    have mercy on us.
Holy Mary,
(after each invocation, respond with,
    "Pray for us")
                        -Pray for us.
Holy Mother of God,
Holy Virgin of virgins,
Mother of Christ,
Mother, full of grace,
Mother most pure,

Mother most chaste,
Immaculate Mother,
Sinless Mother,
Lovable Mother,
Model of mothers,
Mother of good counsel,
Mother of our Maker,
Mother of our Savior,
Wisest of virgins,
Holiest of virgins,
Virgin, powerful in the sight of God,
Virgin, merciful to us sinners,
Virgin, faithful to all God asks of you,
Mirror of holiness,
Seat of wisdom,
Cause of our joy,
Shrine of the Spirit,
Honor of your people,
Devoted handmaid of the Lord,
Tower of David,
Tower of ivory,
House of gold,
Ark of the covenant,

Gate of heaven,
Star of hope,
Health of the sick,
Refuge of sinners,
Comfort of the afflicted,
Help of Christians,
Queen of angels,
Queen of patriarchs,
Queen of prophets,
Queen of apostles,
Queen of martyrs,
Queen of confessors,
Queen of virgins,
Queen of all saints,
Queen conceived in holiness,
Queen raised up to glory,
Queen of the Rosary,
Queen of peace,

Lamb of God, you take away the sins
of the world, – Spare us, O Lord.

Lamb of God, you take away the sins
of the world,

– Graciously hear us, O Lord.

Lamb of God, you take away the sins
of the world,

– Have mercy on us.

Pray for us, O holy Mother of God,

– That we may be made worthy
of the promises of Christ.

Let us pray.

Lord God,

give to your people the joy of
continual health in mind and body.

With the prayers of the Virgin Mary
to help us, guide us through
the sorrows of this life to
eternal happiness in the life to come

We ask this through Christ our Lord.
Amen.

Bartolome Esteban Murillo. *The Madonna of the Rosary*,
Dulwich Picture Gallery, London, UK